THE BEST OF
Chinese
COOKING

Best of Chinese Cooking

Published in the U.K. by
EVANS MITCHELL BOOKS,
17 Manchester Street,
London W1U 4DH.

Edited by Gillian Sutch

ISBN: 1901268-02-0

Design: Centurion Press Ltd., London

Printed and Bound in Hong Kong

THE BEST OF
Chinese COOKING

WILLIE MARK

Evans Mitchell Books

Contents

INTRODUCTION

It would be impossible in a small book to offer a comprehensive look at the multitude of diverse culinary styles that fall under the umbrella of Chinese food. Each region has its own individual style and the robust dishes from Beijing and the colder northern regions and the spicy food from the Western province of Sichuan, to name but two, are each worthy of a separate book. Indeed, the classic cuisine from the southern province of Guangdong, frequently referred to as Cantonese-style cooking and, arguably, the most popular food worldwide could alone offer material to fill many large volumes.

For those unaccustomed to Chinese cooking it can at first appear extremely complicated and time-consuming, but it should be appreciated that most of the effort lies in the preparation. The cooking is usually simple and involves little time which, added to the fact that dishes are generally served simultaneously, makes it an ideal choice for a dinner party. Certainly some dishes are more complicated, but with a little trial and error and, perhaps at the beginning, a certain amount of patience and good humour (surely, essential stand-by 'ingredients' in any kitchen), nothing is impossible.

Family meals in China, while varying from region to region will generally include two or three main courses (fish, poultry or meat), a soup, at least one vegetable dish and the ubiquitous bowl of steaming rice. Naturally, the size of the family, their economical situation and religious beliefs, as well as the availability of local produce will all have a bearing, but it is just this flexibility that adds to the joy of serving a Chinese meal.

For this reason it was not considered practical to indicate a number of servings for each recipe. With a little experimenting and a small amount of improvisation you should soon get the right balance to suit personal circumstances and preferences.

INGREDIENTS

At the time of publication of an earlier edition of this book it was felt necessary to refer to suitable substitutes for a number of ingredients at that time often difficult to obtain outside Asia. However, with the 'globalisation' of eating habits and the variety of ethnic restaurants available throughout the world, it should now not prove difficult to obtain the necessary ingredients to produce a Chinese banquet, let alone a family meal, from most supermarkets throughout Europe and North America. However, if there is a conveniently located Chinese market, a visit will almost certainly provide inspiration for new ideas.

RICE

Rice is a staple food for a large proportion of the world's population and is an essential part of any Chinese meal. At home a large bowl of rice (steamed or boiled) will be placed in the centre of the table, allowing each diner to fill his bowl, and eat along with the other dishes. At more formal dinners, rice, perhaps stir-fried with a mixture of seafood, meat and vegetables, will often be served, as a separate course, towards the end of the meal. A traditional Chinese kitchen (see photograph previous page) would never, in the past, have included a rice cooker, but is nowadays an invaluable asset.

EQUIPMENT

While a well-equipped 'western' kitchen will include everything necessary to prepare a complete and delicious Chinese meal, there is no doubt that certain additional items will make life easier and, consequently, cooking more fun. If the intention is to cook Chinese food frequently, the early purchase of a wok, that most versatile and practical round-based utensil, is highly recommended. Make sure it has a tightly-fitting lid and at the same time purchase a bamboo rack to fit inside. After that, a set of steaming baskets, a pair of long chopsticks and a very sharp cleaver and the kitchen will be well set up.

WEIGHTS AND MEASURES

The recipes have been written using metric measurements with quantities under 75 grams (75 g) and 75 millilitres (75 ml) shown in tablespoons (15 g/ml) and teaspoons (5 g/ml). The bracketed Imperial measures are only approximate conversions.

It should be stressed that Chinese cooks tend not to depend on scales and measuring cups as do many of their Western counterparts and, in particular where spices are concerned, quantities should always be judged to cater for personal tastes.

CHOPSTICKS

Using knives, forks and spoons should not really detract from the enjoyment of eating well-cooked Chinese food although those having mastered the use of chopsticks will almost certainly think otherwise.

At first they may seem awkward and difficult to use but are actually quite simple. Start by gripping one chopstick in a fixed and firm position in the right hand, then take the second one between the thumb and forefinger and manipulate it as you would a pencil. In no time, you will be picking up tiny morsels with ease and will greatly increase the enjoyment of a Chinese meal.

Prawn Dumplings

INGREDIENTS

2 dried Chinese mushrooms
400 g (14 oz) fresh prawns
75 g (3 oz) fat pork
2 water chestnuts, chopped
2 spring onions, chopped
2 tablespoons chopped bamboo shoot
1 tablespoon Chinese wine
2 teaspoons light soy sauce
1 teaspoon dark soy sauce
2 teaspoons sesame oil
freshly ground black pepper
16 won ton wrappers
egg-wash

Soak the mushrooms in warm water for 20 minutes, then discard the hard stems and finely chop the caps.

Shell and de-vein the prawns and chop into small chunks, then combine with the mushroom, pork, chestnut, onion and bamboo shoot and place through a coarse mincer. Add the wine, soy sauce, sesame oil and pepper and mix well.

Lay the won ton wrappers on a lightly greased, flat surface and spoon portions of mixture on to each. Fold into small dumplings, crimp at the top and brush with egg-wash.

Arrange the dumplings in a bamboo basket and steam over rapidly boiling water for 8-10 minutes.

Minced Prawn Balls

INGREDIENTS

450 g (1 lb) fresh prawns
75 g (3 oz) fat pork, chopped
2 teaspoons finely chopped shallot
1 teaspoon finely chopped ginger
1 teaspoon minced garlic
2 teaspoons Chinese wine
1 egg, lightly whisked
salt and pepper to taste
2 tablespoons breadcrumbs
oil for deep frying

Shell and de-vein the prawns and pass through a fine mincer, together with the pork, then combine with the shallot, ginger, garlic, wine, egg, salt and pepper.

Turn on to a lightly-floured surface, shape into small balls and coat with breadcrumbs, then place in the refrigerator for 1 hour. Heat the oil until it starts to smoke, then lower heat slightly and fry the prawn balls, a few at a time until golden and crispy.

Remove with a slotted spoon and drain on kitchen paper, then transfer to a platter and serve immediately.

Sesame Prawn Toast

INGREDIENTS

450 g (1 lb) fresh prawns
1 egg white, lightly beaten
1 teaspoon minced garlic
1 tablespoon light soy sauce
2 teaspoons cornflour
1/2 teaspoon freshly ground pepper
8 slices white bread
2 tablespoons sesame seeds
oil for deep frying

Shell and de-vein the prawns. Pass the prawns through a coarse mincer, then combine with the egg white, garlic, soy sauce, cornflour and pepper to produce a thick, smooth paste.

Cut the crusts off the bread and spread a generous layer of prawn paste on each slice, then sprinkle with sesame seeds.

Heat the oil in a wok until it starts to smoke, then lower heat slightly and deep-fry the prawn slices until crispy and golden.

Remove with a slotted spoon and drain on kitchen paper, then cut into finger slices and serve with a side dip of chilli-vinegar sauce.

Spring Rolls

2 dried Chinese mushrooms
1 teaspoon salt
1 tablespoon sugar
500 ml vegetable oil
125 g (4 oz) fresh baby shrimps
125 g (4 oz) bamboo shoots, shredded
150 g (5 oz) bean sprouts, blanched
125 g (4 oz) roasted pork, shredded
2 tablespoons Chinese wine
1 tablespoon light soy sauce
1 teaspoon dark soy sauce
1 teaspoon sesame oil
freshly ground white pepper
2 teaspoons cornflour
12 spring roll wrappers
egg-wash

Soak the mushrooms in warm water for 20 minutes, then discard the hard stems. Shred the caps and place in a heat-proof bowl. Add salt, 1 teaspoon of sugar and 1 tablespoon of oil and cook in a steamer for 15 minutes. Shell and de-vein the shrimps. Heat 4 tablespoons oil in a wok, add the mushroom and bamboo shoot and stir-fry over a high heat for 1 minute. Add the bean sprouts, pork, shrimps, wine, soy sauce, sesame oil, pepper and remaining sugar and stir for a further 2 minutes. Mix cornflour with a little cold water and stir into the mixture, then leave to cool.

Lay wrappers on a lightly-greased surface and add portions of the mixture. Fold a corner of each wrapper over the mixture, then fold in each side and roll up. Brush with egg-wash. Heat the remaining oil in a wok until it starts to smoke, then lower heat slightly and deep-fry the rolls until golden and crispy. Remove and drain on kitchen paper.

11

Onion Cakes

INGREDIENTS

250 g (9 oz) plain flour
75 g (3 oz) lard, melted
1 teaspoon sugar
1/4 teaspoon salt
1/4 teaspoon freshly ground pepper
1/4 teaspoon Chinese five-spice powder
2 teaspoons sesame oil
8 spring onions, finely chopped
egg-wash
3 tablespoons vegetable oil

Sift the flour into a mixing bowl and add just sufficient boiling water to produce a thick, sticky dough, then cover with a cloth and set aside for 20 minutes. Add the lard, sugar, salt, pepper, five-spice powder and half the sesame oil and knead firmly for 5 minutes, then roll out on a lightly-floured board.

Cover the dough evenly with the spring onion and sprinkle with remaining sesame oil. Shape into a roll, approximately 5 cm (2 inches) in diameter, and cut into 2.5 cm (1 inch) slices, then flatten slightly with the hands. Brush the surface with egg-wash and cook in a steamer for 8-10 minutes, then set aside to cool.

Finally, heat the oil until it starts to smoke, then lower heat slightly and fry the onion cakes for 2-3 minutes, turning once, until golden-brown and crispy.

Taro Dumplings

INGREDIENTS

3 dried Chinese mushrooms
400 g (14 oz) taro root, peeled and sliced
150 g (5 oz) fresh shrimps
125 g (4 oz) chopped lean pork
500 ml (18 fl oz) vegetable oil
salt and freshly ground pepper
1 teaspoon cornflour
3 tablespoons plain flour
75 g (3 oz) lard, melted

Soak the mushrooms in warm water for 20 minutes, then discard the hard stems and dice the caps. Cook the taro in a double boiler until tender, then mash while still hot. Set aside to cool.

Shell and de-vein the shrimps and place through a coarse mincer together with the pork. Heat 2 tablespoons of the oil in a wok and stir-fry the shrimp mixture for 3 minutes, then add the mushroom and season with salt and pepper to taste. Mix the cornflour with a little cold water and stir into the mixture. Cook for a further minute, then set aside to cool.

Sift the flour into a bowl, add the lard, taro and a pinch of salt and mix thoroughly. Knead lightly, then turn on to a lightly-floured surface and shape into a roll. Cut into slices and place a portion of the shrimp mixture in the centre of each. Fold and pinch to seal.

Heat the remaining oil in a large wok and fry the dumplings until golden brown and crispy, then remove and drain on kitchen paper before transferring to a serving platter.

Mandarin Beef

INGREDIENTS

300 g (10 oz) lean beef steak
½ teaspoon salt
¼ teaspoon white pepper
2 eggs, lightly whisked with
  2 teaspoons cornflour
75 ml (3 fl oz) vegetable oil
2 spring onions, chopped
2 teaspoons finely chopped chilli
2 teaspoons finely chopped ginger
1 tablespoon dried mandarin
  peeled, soaked and chopped
1 tablespoon sugar
1 tablespoon light soy sauce
1 teaspoon dark soy sauce
2 tablespoons Chinese wine
2 tablespoons beef stock
1 teaspoon hot sesame oil

Cut the beef into small, thin slices and place in a shallow dish. Season with salt and pepper, add the egg and stir to coat evenly. Set aside for 20 minutes.

Heat half the oil in a wok until it starts to smoke, then lower heat slightly, add the beef and stir-fry for 1 minute, then remove and drain on kitchen paper.

Clean the wok, add remaining oil and reheat, then add onion, chilli, ginger and mandarin peel and stir-fry for 1 minute. Add the sugar, soy sauce, wine and stock and bring to the boil.

Continue to cook until the stock has reduced by three-quarters, then replace the beef, adjust seasonings to taste and stir well.

Cook for a further minute, stirring frequently, then transfer to a serving platter and sprinkle with hot sesame oil.

Barbecued Pork

INGREDIENTS

750 g (1 ¾ lbs) boned pork loin, with skin
2 teaspoons coarse salt
2 teaspoons finely chopped ginger
1 teaspoon finely chopped garlic
2 tablespoons soft brown sugar
2 tablespoons Chinese wine
2 tablespoons light soy sauce
¼ teaspoon red food colouring
125 g (4 oz) clear honey

Score the pork skin with a sharp knife and rub in the salt, then cut the meat into 4 cm (1¾ inch) slices.

Combine the ginger, garlic, sugar, wine, soy sauce and food colouring and rub into the underside of the loin, then set aside for 1 hour.

Thread on skewers, coat with warm honey and cook over very hot charcoal for 25-30 minutes, turning frequently. Coat with the remaining honey at the last minute.

Allow to cool slightly, then cut into thin strips to serve.

Steamed Buns with Barbecued Pork

INGREDIENTS

2 tablespoons vegetable oil
3 spring onions, finely chopped
225 g (8 oz) barbecued pork,
    very finely chopped
2 tablespoons oyster sauce
1 tablespoon light soy sauce
2 teaspoons sugar
1 teaspoon freshly ground pepper
2 tablespoons chicken stock
2 teaspoons cornflour

DOUGH

2 tablespoons sugar
2 teaspoons dried yeast
450 g (1 lb) plain flour
¼ teaspoon salt

Heat the oil in a pan and stir-fry the onion for 2 minutes, then add the pork, oyster sauce, soy sauce, sugar, pepper and stock. Bring to the boil and cook for 3 minutes, stirring frequently. Mix the cornflour with a little cold water and stir into the mixture, then remove from heat and allow to cool.

To make the dough, dissolve the sugar in 100 ml (3 fl oz) of warm water, then stir in the yeast, cover and set aside to ferment for 12-15 minutes.

Sift the flour and salt into a bowl, make a well in the centre and add the fermented yeast. Mix with a wooden spoon, then knead firmly for 5 minutes.

Remove the dough to a lightly-floured surface and shape into a roll, approximately 5 cm (2 inches) in diameter, then cut into 2.5 cm (1 inch) slices and flatten with the hands.

Spoon the pork mixture in the centre of the dough rings, then fold up to form buns. Arrange the buns in a large bamboo basket, cover and steam over rapidly-boiling water for approximately 10 minutes.

Stir-Fried Pork Rolls

INGREDIENTS

300 g (10 oz) pork fillet
$\frac{1}{2}$ teaspoon salt
$\frac{1}{4}$ teaspoon white pepper
1 tablespoon cornflour
1 teaspoon sesame oil
3 flat mushrooms, finely shredded
3 stalks celery, finely shredded
2 tablespoons chopped walnuts
egg-wash
3 tablespoons vegetable oil
2 teaspoons finely chopped ginger
1 teaspoon minced garlic
1 tablespoon chicken stock
2 teaspoons light soy sauce
2 teaspoons sugar

Cut the pork into very thin slices and place in a shallow dish. Sprinkle with salt, pepper, cornflour and sesame oil and set aside for 20 minutes.

Blanch the mushroom and celery and lay 2 shreds on top of each slice of pork. Add a little chopped walnut, then roll up and seal with egg-wash. Heat 2 tablespoons of oil in a wok and fry the pork rolls until cooked through, then remove and drain on kitchen paper. Add the remaining oil and re-heat, then add the ginger and garlic and stir-fry for 2–3 minutes.

Replace the pork rolls, add the stock, soy sauce and sugar and bring to the boil, then lower heat and stir-fry for a further minute. Transfer to a warm platter and serve with a dipping bowl of plum sauce.

Winter Melon Soup

INGREDIENTS

500 g (1¼ lb) winter melon
6 dried Chinese mushrooms
4 water chestnuts
125 g (4 oz) fresh shrimps
1 tablespoon vegetable oil
1 tablespoon finely chopped shallot
2 teaspoons finely chopped ginger
1 teaspoon minced garlic
125 g (4 oz) fresh pork, diced
125 g (4 oz) chicken breast, diced
125 g (4 oz) duck breast, diced
1.75 litres (3 pints) chicken stock
1 tablespoon Chinese wine
1 teaspoon freshly ground pepper
75 g (3 oz) crabmeat, flaked
2 spring onions, finely chopped
1 teaspoon sesame oil
1 tablespoon finely shredded Yunnan ham

Square the bottom of the melon so that it will stand upright. Slice off the top quarter (and retain) and scoop out the seeds and sufficient flesh to allow space for the stock to be added.

Soak the mushrooms in warm water for 20 minutes, then discard the stems and cut the caps into fine strips. Peel and finely chop the water chestnuts. Shell and de-vein the shrimps.

Heat the oil in a saucepan and stir fry the shallot, ginger and garlic for 2 minutes, then add the pork, chicken and duck and cook for a further minute. Pour in the stock and bring to the boil, then add the wine and pepper and allow to simmer for 10 minutes.

Transfer the stock to the melon and cover with the reserved top, then place in a steamer and cook over gently boiling water for 1 hour, then add the shrimps, crabmeat and spring onion and allow to simmer for a further 10 minutes.

To serve, scoop out the flesh from the sides of the melon and place in individual soup bowls, then pour in the stock. Heat the sesame oil and sprinkle on top and garnish with finely shredded Yunnan ham.

Won Ton Soup

INGREDIENTS

- 225 g (8 oz) fresh prawns
- 1/2 teaspoon salt
- 1/4 teaspoon freshly ground pepper
- 1/4 teaspoon sugar
- 1/2 teaspoon cornflour
- 1 teaspoon sesame oil
- 24 won ton wrappers
- egg-wash
- 75 g (3 oz) fresh egg noodles
- 1.5 litres (2 1/2 pints) chicken stock
- 1 tablespoon Chinese wine
- 1 tablespoon light soy sauce
- 2 teaspoons dark soy sauce
- 2 spring onions, finely chopped

Shell and de-vein the prawns chop finely. Place in shallow dish, add salt, pepper, sugar and cornflour and mix well, then sprinkle with sesame oil and set aside for 20 minutes.

Lay the won ton wrappers on a lightly greased surface and place a little of the prawn paste in the centre of each. Fold up like a string purse and crimp at the top to secure, then brush with egg-wash and place in the refrigerator for at least 30 minutes.

Cook the noodles in rapidly boiling water for 2-3 minutes, then strain, rinse under cold water and strain again. Bring the stock to the boil, then add the wine and soy sauce. Add the noodles and cook for 30 seconds, then remove, strain and transfer to individual soup bowls.

Bring stock back to the boil, add the won tons and cook until they float to the surface, then remove won tons and transfer to the soup bowls. Add the spring onions to the stock, boil for a further minute, then pour into the bowls and serve immediately.

Crabmeat and Sweetcorn Soup

INGREDIENTS

250 g (9 oz) cooked crabmeat
2 tablespoons Chinese wine
1 teaspoon sesame oil
salt to taste
freshly ground black pepper
2 tablespoons cornflour
1.25 litres (2 pints) chicken stock
275 g (10 oz) can sweetcorn, drained
2 eggs, lightly whisked
2 tablespoons finely chopped Yunnan ham
1 teaspoon freshly chopped coriander

Flake the crabmeat and place in a shallow dish. Mix the wine with the sesame oil, salt, pepper and half the cornflour and pour over the crab. Set aside for 15 minutes.

Pour the chicken stock into a saucepan, add the corn and bring slowly to the boil, then lower heat and simmer for 2-3 minutes. Add the crabmeat, bring back to the boil and cook for a further minute.

Mix remaining cornflour with a little cold water and add to the soup to thicken slightly.

Add the egg, stirring continuously until it starts to set in threads, then transfer to a tureen and garnish with ham and coriander.

Seafood and Bean Curd Soup

INGREDIENTS

100 g (4 oz) shrimps
100 g (4 oz) cooked crabmeat
1 egg
2 teaspoons light soy sauce
1 teaspoon sesame oil
freshly ground black pepper
2 tablespoons cornflour
1.5 litres (2 1/4 pints) chicken stock
225 g (8 oz) fresh bean curd,
    cut into small bite-size pieces
1 tablespoon shredded ginger
100 g (4 oz) firm white fish fillet,
    cut into small chunks
1 spring onion, thinly sliced
salt to taste
2 tablespoons Chinese wine
2 teaspoons freshly chopped coriander

Shell and de-vein the shrimps and flake the crabmeat. Break the egg into a bowl, add the soy sauce, sesame oil, pepper and 2 teaspoons cornflour and whisk lightly. Pour half the mixture over the shrimps and the remainder over the crabmeat and set both aside for 20 minutes.

Pour the stock into a saucepan and bring to the boil. Add the bean curd and ginger and boil for 1 minute, then add the white fish and cook for a further minute.

Add the shrimps, crabmeat and spring onion and stir well, then season with salt to taste and bring back to the boil.

Mix the remaining cornflour with a little cold water and add to the soup to thicken slightly, then transfer to a tureen. Add the wine and stir well, then garnish with coriander and serve immediately.

Raw Fish Soup

INGREDIENTS

350 g (12 oz) white fish fillets
1 tablespoon olive oil
2 shallots, thinly sliced
1 tablespoon finely chopped ginger
4 lettuce leaves, shredded
$^{1}/_{2}$ teaspoon sesame oil
1 litre (2 $^{1}/_{4}$ pints) fish stock
salt to taste
freshly ground white pepper
freshly chopped parsley

Remove the skin from the fish fillets, ensure no small bones remain, and cut the meat into thin slices.

Heat the oil in a small pan and sauté the shallot and ginger for 2–3 minutes, then remove and drain on kitchen paper.

Place the shredded lettuce in the bottom of a soup tureen, then add the shallot, ginger and fish and sprinkle with sesame oil.

Bring the stock to the boil and season with salt and pepper, then pour over the fish and garnish with freshly chopped parsley. Serve immediately.

Shark's Fin and Crabmeat Soup

INGREDIENTS

450 g (1 lb) shark's fin
2 spring onions, sliced
8 thin slices fresh ginger
2 tablespoons Chinese wine
2 tablespoons finely shredded Yunnan ham
1.5 litres (2 ½ pints) chicken stock
4 crab claws
4 small asparagus spears
1 tablespoon light soy sauce
1 teaspoon dark soy sauce
½ teaspoon white pepper

Place the shark's fin in a pan and add sufficient cold water to cover. Soak for 12 hours, then transfer to a pan of boiling water and add the onion, ginger and wine.

Lower heat and allow to simmer for 5-6 hours, then remove pan from heat, cover and allow to stand for 1 hour. Drain the shark's fin and transfer to a large tureen and sprinkle the ham on top.

Bring the stock to the boil and pour into the tureen, then cover, place on a rack and steam over rapidly boiling water for 45 minutes.

Meanwhile, crack the crab claws and steam for 10 minutes, then carefully remove shells, leaving the meat in one piece.

Cook the asparagus until tender, then cut each spear in half. Add to the tureen together with the crabmeat, then season with soy sauce and pepper and continue to steam for a further 5 minutes. Serve immediately.

Chicken and Sweetcorn soup

INGREDIENTS

200 g (7 oz) chicken breast fillets
¼ teaspoon salt
freshly ground black pepper
2 eggs, lightly beaten
1 tablespoon vegetable oil
1.25 litres (2 pints) chicken stock
275 g (9 oz) can sweetcorn, drained
1 tablespoon light soy sauce
1 teaspoon dark soy sauce
1 tablespoon Chinese wine
1 tablespoon finely chopped parsley

Skin the chicken breasts, cut the meat into small dice and place in a shallow dish. Season with salt and pepper, add half the beaten egg and stir to coat evenly, then set aside for 20 minutes.

Heat the oil in a large pan, add the chicken and stir for 5 minutes, then add the stock and bring to the boil. Add the sweetcorn and simmer for 3 minutes, then add the soy sauce and wine.

Add the remaining egg and stir for 2 minutes, then transfer to a soup tureen and sprinkle with chopped parsley. Serve immediately.

Chicken Liver and Ginger Soup

INGREDIENTS

3 dried Chinese mushrooms
200 g (7 oz) chicken livers
75 g (3 oz) chicken giblets
1/4 teaspoon salt
2 tablespoons peanut oil
8 thin slices of fresh ginger
1 spring onion, chopped
1 litre (2 1/4 pints) chicken stock
2 tablespoons Chinese wine
1 tablespoon light soy sauce
1 teaspoon dark soy sauce
freshly ground black pepper
fresh coriander leaves

Soak the mushrooms in warm water for 20 minutes, then discard the hard stems and slice the caps.

Wash and prepare the livers and blanch in boiling water for 2 minutes, then slice and set aside. Bring the water back to the boil, add the giblets and salt and cook for 15 minutes, then strain and discard the giblets. Reserve 250 ml (8 fl oz) of the water.

Heat the oil in a saucepan, and stir-fry the ginger for 3 minutes, then add the liver, mushroom and the spring onion and stir for a further minute.

Add the stock and reserved water and bring to the boil, then add the wine, soy sauce and pepper. Lower heat and allow to simmer for 10 minutes, then transfer to a soup tureen and float fresh coriander leaves on top.

Pork Liver and Tomato Soup

INGREDIENTS

175 g (6 oz) pork liver
1 tablespoon finely chopped ginger
1 tablespoon finely chopped spring onion
2 tablespoons light soy sauce
2 teaspoons dark soy sauce
2 teaspoons sugar
1 tablespoon cornflour
1.5 litres (2 1/2 pints) chicken stock
3 large tomatoes, thinly sliced
2 tablespoons vegetable oil
1 tablespoon Chinese wine
freshly ground black pepper

Soak the liver in cold water for 30 minutes, then pat dry and cut into small, thin slices. Combine the ginger, onion, soy sauce, sugar, cornflour and 3 tablespoons stock. Add the liver and stir to coat evenly, then set aside for 30 minutes.

Pour remaining stock into a saucepan and bring to the boil. Add the tomato, lower heat and allow to simmer for 10 minutes.

Meanwhile, heat the oil in a wok, add the liver, together with marinade and stir-fry for 3 minutes. Remove and drain on kitchen paper, then add to the stock and bring back to a simmer. Cook for a further 3 minutes, then stir in the wine and transfer to a soup tureen. Add a good grinding of black pepper and serve immediately.

Hot and Sour Soup

INGREDIENTS

4 dried Chinese mushrooms
150 g (5 oz) fresh prawns
2 tablespoons vegetable oil
125 g (4 oz) roasted pork, finely shredded
75 g (3 oz) bamboo shoot, shredded
75 g (3 oz) cucumber, shredded
4 fresh red chillies, finely chopped
1 tablespoon finely chopped ginger
100 g (4 oz) fresh bean curd, diced
1.5 litres (2 ½ pints) chicken stock
2 teaspoons light soy sauce
1 teaspoon dark soy sauce
1 tablespoon Chinese wine
1 tablespoon vinegar
1 teaspoon freshly ground pepper
2 teaspoon cornflour
1 egg, lightly beaten
1 teaspoon chilli oil

Soak the mushrooms in warm water for 20 minutes, then discard the hard stems and shred the caps. Shell and de-vein the prawns and cut in half, lengthways.

Heat the oil in a large pan, add the mushroom, prawn, pork, bamboo shoot, cucumber, chilli, ginger and bean curd and stir-fry for 2 minutes, then pour in the stock and bring to the boil. Continue to boil for 1 minute, then lower heat, add soy sauce, wine, vinegar and pepper and allow to simmer for a further 3-4 minutes.

Mix the cornflour with a small quantity of cold water and stir into the soup to thicken slightly. Add the egg and stir until it starts to set in thin threads, then transfer to a soup tureen. Finally, heat the chilli oil and sprinkle over the soup.

Braised Crab with Ginger

INGREDIENTS

2 fresh crabs

3 tablespoons cornflour

oil for deep frying

2 tablespoons grated ginger

1 teaspoon minced garlic

2 shallots, finely chopped

250 ml (8 fl oz) chicken stock

1 tablespoon Chinese wine

2 teaspoons dark soy sauce

1 teaspoon sugar

salt and pepper to taste

1 teaspoon hot sesame oil

Prepare the crabs, break off of the claws and chop the body into serving size pieces. Dust with 1 tablespoon cornflour.

Heat the oil in a wok and fry the crab for 2 minutes, then remove and drain on kitchen paper. Pour away most of the oil, reheat the wok and stir-fry the ginger, garlic and shallot for 1 minute, then add the stock, wine and soy sauce and bring to the boil. Replace the crab, season with sugar, salt and pepper and cover the wok, then continue to cook for 5-6 minutes.

Finally, mix the remaining cornflour with a little water and stir into the sauce to thicken slightly, then transfer to a serving dish and sprinkle with hot sesame oil.

Crab Claws with Shrimp Paste

INGREDIENTS

8 fresh crab claws

175 fresh shrimps

100 g (4 oz) pork fat

1 egg-white, lightly whisked

1 teaspoon sugar

1/4 teaspoon salt

1/4 teaspoon white pepper

1 tablespoon light soy sauce

1 teaspoon dark soy sauce

1 teaspoon sesame oil

2 tablespoons cornflour

vegetable oil for frying

Crack the crab claws and cook in a steamer then carefully remove the shell, leaving the claw meat intact and still attached to the 'nipper'.

Shell and de-vein the shrimps and pass though a fine mincer, together with the pork, then add the egg, sugar, salt, pepper, soy sauce, sesame oil, half the cornflour and a little cold water to produce a sticky paste. Mould the mixture around the crab claws and dust with the remaining cornflour. Heat the oil in a wok until it starts to smoke, then add the crab claws and cook until golden and crispy, then remove and drain on kitchen paper before transferring to a serving dish.

Crab in Black Bean Sauce

INGREDIENTS

2 large crabs

1 egg white, lightly beaten with

  2 teaspoons dark soy sauce

  $\frac{1}{2}$ teaspoon white pepper

  2 teaspoons cornflour

1 tablespoon fermented black beans

2 tablespoons peanut oil

3 tablespoons vegetable oil

1 onion, finely chopped

1 green pepper, finely chopped

1 tablespoon finely chopped ginger

2 teaspoons minced garlic

1 teaspoon sugar

1 tablespoon Chinese wine

1 tablespoon light soy sauce

1 teaspoon sesame oil

125 ml (5 fl oz) chicken stock

2 teaspoons cornflour

Boil the crabs, then allow to cool. Remove all the meat and place in a mixing bowl. Add the egg, stir and set aside.

Mash the fermented beans with the peanut oil to produce a smooth paste.

Heat the vegetable oil in a wok until it starts to smoke, then lower heat slightly and stir-fry the crabmeat for 1 minute. Add the onion and green pepper and stir for a further 2 minutes, then remove with a slotted spoon and drain on kitchen paper.

Pour away most of the oil and reheat the wok, then add the ginger and garlic. Stir-fry for 2 minutes, then add the black bean paste and stir for a further minute.

Add the sugar, wine, soy sauce, sesame oil and stock and bring to the boil, then replace the crabmeat and vegetables and adjust seasonings to taste.

Finally, mix the cornflour with a little cold water and stir into the sauce to thicken slightly, then transfer to a warm platter

Stir-Fried Prawns with Choi Sum

INGREDIENTS

8 fresh king prawns
1 egg white, lightly beaten with
  2 teaspoons cornflour
  1 teaspoon sugar
  ½ teaspoon salt
  ¼ teaspoon white pepper
3 tablespoons vegetable oil
300 g choi sum, trimmed
2 tablespoons chicken stock
2 teaspoons Chinese wine
1 teaspoon oyster sauce
2 teaspoons finely chopped ham

Shell and de-vein the prawns and place in a shallow dish. Add the beaten egg and stir to coat evenly, then set aside for 30 minutes.

Heat half the oil in a wok until it starts to smoke, then lower heat and add the choi sum, salt and pepper. Stir-fry for 2 minutes, then remove and drain on kitchen paper.

Add the remaining oil to the wok and stir-fry the prawns over a high heat for 30 seconds, then remove and drain.

Add the stock wine and oyster sauce to the wok and bring to the boil, the replace the prawns and choi sum and adjust seasonings to taste.

Cook for a further minute, then arrange on a serving plate and sprinkle the ham on top.

Sesame Prawns

INGREDIENTS

12 fresh king prawns
2 spring onions, finely chopped
1 fresh red chilli, finely chopped
1 teaspoon shredded ginger
1 teaspoon minced garlic
75 ml (3 fl oz) Chinese wine
1 tablespoon light soy sauce
1 teaspoon sugar
1/4 teaspoon freshly ground pepper
egg-wash
2 tablespoons plain flour
2 teaspoons sesame seeds
oil for deep frying
fresh sprigs of parsley

Shell and de-vein the prawns, leaving tails intact. With a sharp knife, slit the prawns along the back, three quarters of the way through, then flatten out in butterfly style and place in a shallow dish.

Mix together the onion, chilli, ginger, garlic, wine, soy sauce, sugar and pepper and pour over the prawns. Set aside for 20 minutes, turning the prawns once. Dip the prawns in the egg-wash and dust with flour, then dip in sesame seeds.

Heat the oil in a wok until very hot and deep-fry the prawns until golden and crispy. Remove and drain on kitchen paper, then transfer to a serving plate and garnish with sprigs of parsley.

Prawn Cutlets

INGREDIENTS

12 fresh king prawns
salt and freshly ground pepper
2 tablespoons Chinese wine
4 eggs, lightly beaten with
   2 tablespoons cornflour
3 tablespoons fine breadcrumbs

Shell and de-vein the prawns, leaving tails intact. With a sharp knife, slit the prawns along the back, three-quarters of the way through, then flatten out in butterfly style. Sprinkle with salt, pepper and wine and set aside for 10 minutes, then dip in the beaten egg and coat with breadcrumbs.

Heat the oil until it starts to smoke, then lower heat slightly and deep-fry the prawns until golden and crispy. Drain off excess oil, then transfer to a platter and serve with a side dip of shredded chillies in vinegar.

Stir-Fried Lobster

INGREDIENTS

2 fresh lobsters, approximately
   600 g (1 1/4 lbs) each
salt and freshly ground pepper
2 teaspoons cornflour
100 ml (4 fl oz) peanut oil
2 teaspoons finely chopped ginger
1 teaspoon finely chopped garlic
2 spring onions, finely sliced
3 tablespoons Chinese wine
2 teaspoons light soy sauce
1 teaspoon sugar
200 ml (8 fl oz) clear fish stock
sprig of fresh coriander

Boil the lobsters and allow to cool, then break off the tail, crack the claws and carefully remove all the meat. Cut the meat into small chunks, season with salt and pepper and dust with cornflour.

Heat the oil in a wok and stir-fry the lobster for 1 minute, then remove and drain on kitchen paper.

Pour away most of the oil and reheat the wok. Add the ginger and garlic and stir-fry for 3 minutes, then add the spring onion and cook for a further minute.

Replace the lobster, add the wine, soy sauce, sugar and stock and bring to the boil, then lower heat and adjust seasonings to taste. Simmer for a further minute, then transfer to a warm serving plate and garnish with fresh coriander.

Lobster Omelette

INGREDIENTS

350 g (12 oz) cooked lobster meat
salt and freshly ground pepper
3 tablespoons peanut oil
1 tablespoon finely chopped ginger
1 teaspoon minced garlic
2 spring onions, finely sliced
2 tablespoon finely chopped green pepper
2 tablespoons Chinese wine
1 tablespoon light soy sauce
8 eggs, lightly beaten
1 teaspoon sesame oil
1 teaspoon freshly chopped coriander

Chop the lobster meat into small chunks and season with salt and pepper.

Heat 1 tablespoon of oil in a wok and stir-fry the ginger and garlic for 3 minutes, then add the lobster, spring onion, green pepper, wine and soy sauce. Stir well and bring to the boil.

Lower heat and cook for 2 minutes, then adjust seasonings to taste and transfer to a mixing bowl. Allow to cool slightly, then add the egg and sesame oil and stir to blend thoroughly.

Heat the remaining oil in a clean wok and pour in the mixture. Cook over a moderate heat, turning and breaking up, until the egg is set softly, then transfer to a warm platter and serve immediately.

Sweet and Sour Fish

INGREDIENTS

750 g (1 ¾ lb) whole fish
½ teaspoon salt
¼ teaspoon white pepper
1 egg, lightly whisked with
   2 teaspoons cornflour
oil for deep frying

SAUCE

1 tablespoon peanut oil
1 onion, coarsely chopped
1 green pepper, coarsely chopped
2 teaspoons finely chopped chilli
2 teaspoons finely chopped ginger
1 teaspoon finely chopped garlic
125 g (4 oz) tin pineapple chunks
2 tablespoons Chinese wine
2 tablespoons light soy sauce
2 tablespoons vinegar
75 ml (3 fl oz) clear fish stock
2 tablespoons sugar
2 teaspoons cornflour

Prepare the fish, leaving the head and tail attached. Score the skin in several places and rub in the salt and pepper, then place in a dish and add the egg. Set aside for 20 minutes.

Heat the oil in a wok until it starts to smoke, then lower heat and fry the fish for 4-5 minutes, until fully cooked and the skin is golden and crispy. Remove and drain on kitchen paper, then transfer to a serving plate and coat with sauce.

To make the sauce, heat the oil in a pan, add the onion, pepper, chilli, ginger and garlic and stir-fry for 2-3 minutes, then add the pineapple, wine, soy sauce, vinegar, stock and sugar and bring to the boil.

Stir until the sugar has dissolved, then lower heat and allow to simmer for a further minute. Finally, mix the cornflour with a little cold water and stir in to the sauce to thicken slightly.

Garoupa with Ham and Mushrooms

INGREDIENTS

600 g (1 ¼ lbs) garoupa fillets
8 dried Chinese mushrooms
100 g (4 oz) slices of Yunnan ham
4 spring onions, sliced
salt and pepper to taste
1 tablespoon vegetable oil
2 teaspoons finely chopped ginger
1 teaspoon finely chopped garlic
100 ml (4 fl oz) chicken stock
1 tablespoon light soy sauce
1 tablespoon Chinese wine
2 teaspoons sesame oil
freshly ground black pepper
2 teaspoons cornflour

Cut the fish, diagonally, into slices, approximately 15 mm (½ inch) thick. Soak the mushrooms in warm water for 20 minutes, then discard the hard stems and halve the caps. Soak the ham in warm water for 15 minutes, then pat dry and cut into thin strips.

Place the spring onion in the bottom of a shallow, ovenproof dish and add alternating pieces of fish, ham and mushrooms. Season with salt and pepper, then set the dish on a bamboo rack, place in a steamer and cook over rapidly boiling water for 4-5 minutes. Heat the oil in a wok, add the ginger and garlic and stir-fry for 2 minutes, then add the stock, soy sauce, wine, sesame oil and pepper and bring to the boil. Allow to simmer for 1 minute.

Finally, mix the cornflour with a small quantity of cold water and stir into the sauce to thicken slightly, then pour over the fish and serve immediately.

Fish in Wine Sauce

INGREDIENTS

500 g (1 1/4 lb) white fish fillets
salt and pepper
1 egg white
2 teaspoon dark soy sauce
1 tablespoon cornflour
75 g (3 oz) dried wood-ear mushrooms
oil for deep frying
2 teaspoons sugar
3 tablespoons Chinese wine
125 ml (4 fl oz) clear fish stock

Cut the fish into serving-size pieces, place in a shallow dish and season with salt and pepper. Whisk the egg white with the soy sauce and half the cornflour and pour over the fish. Stir to coat evenly and set aside for 30 minutes.

Soak the wood-ear mushrooms in warm water for 20 minutes, then rinse under cold running water and pat dry.

Heat the oil in a wok until it starts to smoke and fry the fish for 45 seconds, then remove with a slotted spoon and drain on kitchen paper. Pour away most of the oil and stir-fry the mushrooms for 2 minutes, then add the sugar, wine and stock and bring to the boil.

Mix the remaining cornflour with a small quantity of cold water and stir into the sauce, then replace fish and cook for a further 3-4 minutes.

Pomfret, Chiu Chow Style

INGREDIENTS

1 whole pomfret,
  approximately 900 g (2 lbs)
2 dried Chinese mushrooms
4 spring onions, finely sliced
2 stalks celery, shredded
2 pickled plums, shredded
1 tablespoon finely sliced ginger
2 teaspoons finely chopped Yunnan ham
8 fresh coriander leaves
100 ml (3 fl oz) chicken stock
2 tablespoons hot peanut oil

Prepare the fish, then wash under cold running water and pat dry. Soak the mushrooms in warm water for 20 minutes, then discard the hard stems and shred the caps.

Line the base of a shallow dish with the spring onion and lay the fish on top. Arrange the mushroom, celery, pickled plum, ginger, ham and coriander leaves on top of the fish and add the stock. Place the dish on a bamboo steaming rack.

Pour a little water into a wok and bring to the boil. Place the rack in the wok, ensuring it remains about 20 mm (¾ inch) above the level of the water.

Place a tightly fitting lid on the wok and steam the fish for 10–12 minutes, then transfer to a serving dish and sprinkle with hot peanut oil. Serve immediately.

Spicy Steamed Pomfret

INGREDIENTS

1 whole pomfret
   approximately 800 g (1 $^3/_4$ lbs)
$^1/_4$ teaspoon salt
$^1/_4$ teaspoon black pepper
3 spring onions, chopped
3 fresh red chillies, finely sliced
1 tablespoon finely chopped ginger
1 teaspoon finely chopped garlic
2 tablespoons fermented black beans
$^1/_4$ teaspoon hot mustard powder
2 teaspoons sugar
2 tablespoons Chinese wine
1 tablespoon light soy sauce
2 tablespoons clear fish stock
75 ml (3 fl oz) peanut oil
2 teaspoons freshly chopped coriander

Prepare the fish and make a number of incisions along each side. Rub the salt and pepper into the fish and set aside for 20 minutes.

Lay the spring onions in the base of a shallow, heatproof dish and lay the fish on top. Combine the chilli, ginger, garlic, black beans, mustard, sugar, wine, soy sauce and stock and pour over the fish.

Place the fish in a steamer and cook for 8-10 minutes, then transfer to a serving plate. Heat the oil and sprinkle over the fish, then garnish with freshly chopped coriander.

Smoked Pomfret

INGREDIENTS

650 g (1 1/2 lb) whole pomfret
1 tablespoon finely chopped ginger
3 spring onions, finely chopped
2 tablespoons Chinese wine
2 tablespoons light soy sauce
1 teaspoon ground anise
1 teaspoon sugar
175 g (6 oz) rice
75 g (3 oz) plain flour
3 tablespoons dried tea leaves
2 teaspoons sesame oil
sprigs of fresh parsley

Prepare the fish and, with a sharp knife, score in a criss-cross fashion along both sides. Combine half the ginger and half the spring onion with the wine and soy sauce and rub the mixture into the flesh of the fish. Set aside for 30 minutes, then cook in a steamer for 5 minutes.

Combine the remaining ginger and spring onion with the anise, sugar, rice, flour and tea leaves and place in the bottom of a wok. Arrange a bamboo rack in the wok, approximately 25 mm (1 inch) above the mixture and place on a high heat. When it starts to smoke, place the fish on the rack and cover the wok with a tightly fitting lid.

Allow to smoke for 2-3 minutes, then transfer the fish to a warm platter, sprinkle with hot sesame oil and garnish with sprigs of fresh parsley.

Crispy Fried Eel

INGREDIENTS

675 g (1 ¹/₂ lb) fresh water eel
1 brown onion, finely chopped
1 carrot, finely chopped
1 stalk celery, finely chopped
1 tablespoon finely chopped
  coriander leaves
1 tablespoon oyster sauce
1 teaspoon dark soy sauce
1 teaspoon salt
¹/₂ teaspoon freshly ground pepper
2 tablespoons Chinese wine
2 tablespoons cornflour
oil for deep frying
fresh lemon slices

Wash the eel in hot water, then pat dry and cut into slivers, about 15 mm (¹/₂ inch) thick. Place in a shallow dish.

Place the onion, carrot, celery and coriander in a small saucepan and cover with 125 ml (4 fl oz) water. Bring to the boil and reduce the liquid by two-thirds, then add the oyster sauce, soy sauce, salt, pepper and half the wine. Mix well, then pour over the eel and stir to coat evenly. Place in the refrigerator for 2 hours, then remove eel and dust with the cornflour.

Heat the oil in a wok and carefully add the eel, one sliver at a time to avoid them sticking together. Cook for 2 minutes, then remove with a slotted spoon and drain on kitchen paper.

Increase the heat until the oil starts to smoke, then replace the eel and cook for a further 30 seconds until golden and crispy. Remove with a slotted spoon and drain off excess oil, then transfer to a platter and garnish with slices of fresh lemon.

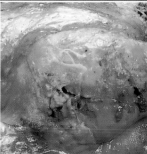

Peking Duck

INGREDIENTS

1 fat duck, approx. 2.5 kilos
1 tablespoon salt
2 teaspoons Chinese five-spice powder
125 ml golden syrup
2 tablespoons honey
2 tablespoons light soy sauce
6 spring onions cut into
  5 cm (2 inch) lengths
1 small cucumber, cut into thin sticks
100 ml (4 oz) plum sauce

PANCAKES

500 g (1 lb) plain flour
½ teaspoon salt
75 ml (3 fl oz) sesame oil

Clean and prepare the duck. Cut off the feet but leave on the head. Immerse the duck in a pan of rapidly boiling water for a few seconds, then remove and pat dry. Rub the salt and five-spice powder inside the duck.

Mix the syrup, honey and soy sauce with a small quantity of water and bring to the boil, then coat the duck, inside and out, with the syrup mixture. Place a string around the neck and hang in a cool, draughty place for 4–5 hours to stretch the skin. Place the duck in a moderately hot oven and cook for 2 hours, or until the duck is tender and the skin is crispy and golden, then carve off pieces of skin and arrange on a platter.

To serve, place a piece of duck on a pancake, add a piece of spring onion and cucumber and top with a little plum sauce. Fold the pancake over the duck and tuck in ends to secure.

To make the pancakes, sift the flour and salt into a bowl and make a well in the centre. Add approximately 400 ml (14 fl oz) boiling water, a little at a time, and mix to form a soft dough. Knead gently for 10 minutes until the dough becomes pliable, then cover and allow to stand for 20–25 minutes.

Turn out on to a lightly floured surface and shape into a cylinder, approximately 5 cm (2 inches) in diameter, then cut into circles, approximately 5 mm (⅛ inch) thick. Brush one side of each circle with sesame oil and place two together with the oiled sides facing, then roll out until approximately 15 cm (6 inches) in diameter. Heat a heavy pan and cook a pair of pancakes for 30–45 seconds on each side, then peel apart and stack on a warm plate until all the pancakes have been cooked.

Stuffed Duckling

INGREDIENTS

1.25 kilo (3 lb) fresh duckling
oil for deep frying
1 large onion, coarsely chopped
1 tablespoon chopped ginger
1 tablespoon chopped orange rind
300 g (10 oz) minced lamb
2 teaspoons finely chopped lemon grass
2 teaspoons sugar
1/2 teaspoon salt
1/4 teaspoon back pepper
2 teaspoons dark soy sauce

Prepare the duckling, wash under cold water and hang to dry in the air for 3 hours. Heat the oil in a wok until very hot and deep-fry the duck for 5 minutes, then remove, drain off excess oil, place in a large saucepan and cover with near-boiling water. Add the onion, ginger and orange rind and simmer for 1 hour, then remove and drain. Allow to cool, then cut carefully remove all the bones.

Combine the lamb, lemon grass, sugar, salt, pepper and soy sauce and stuff into the cavity of the duck. Secure openings with kitchen thread and wrap with thin strips of foil to maintain the shape.

Reheat the oil in the wok until it starts to smoke, then lower heat slightly, add the duck and deep-fry for 12-15 minutes until the skin is golden and crispy. Remove and drain, then cut into bite-size pieces and arrange on a serving platter.

Lemon Duck

INGREDIENTS

4 duck breast fillets
4 egg yolks, lightly beaten
3 shallots, finely chopped
2 teaspoons finely chopped ginger
1 tablespoon light soy sauce
1 teaspoon dark soy sauce
2 tablespoons cornflour
oil for deep frying
fresh lemon slices

SAUCE

2 tablespoons butter
2 tablespoons rice flour
100 ml (4 fl oz) fresh lemon juice
100 ml (4 fl oz) chicken stock
2 tablespoons Chinese wine
1 tablespoon sugar
2 teaspoons cornflour

Remove the skin from the duck fillets
and cut the meat into bite-size pieces.
Mix together the egg yolks, shallots,
ginger, soy sauce and half the cornflour
and pour over the duck. Set aside in a
cool place for 1 hour, then dust with
the remaining cornflour.

Heat the oil in a wok until it starts to
smoke. Lower heat slightly, add the duck
and cook until tender and crispy, then
remove and drain on kitchen paper.
Arrange the duck on a platter, pour on
the sauce and garnish with fresh lemon
slices.

To make the sauce, melt the butter in a
saucepan, then remove pan from heat and
stir in the flour. Return pan to the heat,
add the lemon juice and stock and bring
to the boil, then add the wine and sugar
and stir to blend. Finally, mix the
cornflour with a small quantity of cold
water and stir into the sauce to thicken
slightly.

Chicken in Black Bean Sauce

INGREDIENTS

1 whole chicken
$\frac{1}{2}$ teaspoon salt
freshly ground black pepper
2 teaspoons Chinese wine
oil for deep frying
150 g (5 oz) shallots, sliced
1 green pepper, chopped
2 teaspoons finely chopped garlic
1 teaspoon finely chopped orange peel
1 tablespoon preserved black beans
2 teaspoons sugar
1 tablespoon light soy sauce
2 teaspoons dark soy sauce
150 ml (5 fl oz) chicken stock
2 teaspoons cornflour
fresh coriander leaves

Joint the chicken, remove the bones and skin and cut the meat into bite-size pieces, then season with salt, pepper and wine and set aside for 20 minutes.

Heat the oil in a wok and deep fry the chicken pieces until tender and golden, then remove with a slotted spoon and drain on kitchen paper.

Pour away most of the oil and replace the wok over a high heat. Add the shallot, green pepper and garlic and stir-fry for 3 minutes, then add the orange peel, black beans, sugar, soy sauce and stock and bring to the boil.

Cook for a further 2 minutes, then replace the chicken and stir well. Mix the cornflour with a little cold water and stir into the sauce to thicken slightly, then transfer to a serving dish and garnish with fresh coriander leaves.

Chicken with Dried Chillies

INGREDIENTS

450 g (1 lb) chicken meat
$\frac{1}{2}$ teaspoon salt
$\frac{1}{4}$ teaspoon white pepper
$\frac{1}{4}$ teaspoon five-spice powder
2 tablespoons cornflour
250 g (9 oz) dried red chillies
75 ml (3 fl oz) vegetable oil
1 tablespoon finely chopped shallot
1 tablespoon finely chopped ginger
2 teaspoons finely chopped garlic
2 tablespoons Chinese wine
1 tablespoon light soy sauce
2 teaspoons dark soy sauce
1 tablespoon vinegar
2 teaspoons sugar
2 teaspoons sesame oil
3 fresh red chillies, finely sliced

Cut the chicken meat into bite-size pieces and place in a shallow dish, then season with salt, pepper and five-spice powder. Mix the cornflour with 75 ml (3 fl oz) of cold water and pour over the chicken, then set aside for 20 minutes.

Trim the dried chillies, slice lengthways and remove most of the seeds. Heat 3 tablespoons of oil in a wok, add the shallot, ginger and garlic and stir-fry for 2 minutes, then add the chicken and stir for a further minute. Remove and set aside.

Clean the wok, add the remaining oil and place over a high heat until the oil starts to smoke. Add the chillies and stir until they start to blacken, then lower heat and replace the chicken. Add the wine, soy sauce, vinegar and sugar and continue to cook for 2-3 minutes, stirring frequently, then remove the pieces of chicken and place in a serving dish. Heat the sesame oil and sprinkle over the chicken, then garnish with freshly sliced chilli.

Note: The kitchen should be well ventilated when cooking this dish as the dried chillies give off a powerful smell which gets deep into the throat, and may cause discomfort for some.

Chicken Breasts with Peppers

INGREDIENTS

4 boneless chicken breasts

2 egg whites

2 tablespoons Chinese wine

2 teaspoons dark soy sauce

1 teaspoon sugar

salt and pepper to taste

75 ml (3 fl oz) vegetable oil

1 small red pepper, shredded

1 small green pepper, shredded

2 teaspoons finely chopped ginger

1 teaspoon finely chopped garlic

1 tablespoon light soy sauce

1 tablespoon oyster sauce

75 ml (3 fl oz) chicken stock

2 teaspoons cornflour

Flatten the chicken breasts slightly with a kitchen mallet and lay in a shallow dish. Beat egg whites with half the wine, soy sauce, sugar, salt and pepper and pour over the chicken, then turn to coat evenly and set aside for 30 minutes.

Heat half the oil in a wok and fry the chicken for 2–3 minutes on each side, then remove to a serving dish and keep warm.

Add half the remaining oil to the wok and stir-fry the peppers for 2 minutes, then remove and arrange on top of the chicken. Add remaining oil and stir-fry the ginger and garlic for 2 minutes, then add the oyster sauce, stock and remaining wine and bring to the boil.

Lower heat and allow to simmer for 2 minutes, then mix the cornflour with a small quantity of cold water and add to the sauce. Stir for a further minute for sauce to thicken slightly, then pour around the chicken and serve immediately.

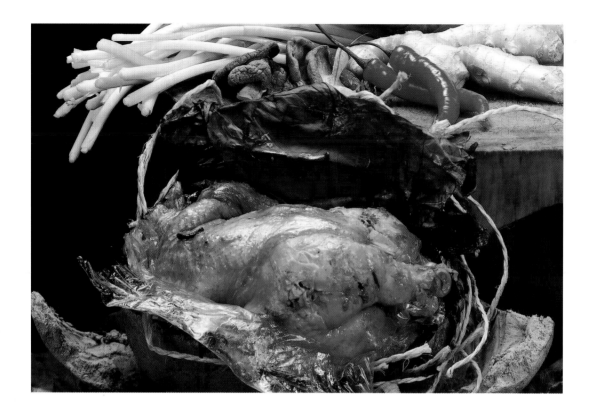

Beggar's Chicken

INGREDIENTS

- 1.5 kilos (3 ¼ lb) whole chicken
- 2 teaspoons salt
- 6 dried Chinese mushrooms
- 2 tablespoons vegetable oil
- 125 g (4 oz) minced pork
- 125 g (4 oz) pickled cabbage, shredded
- 125 g (4 oz) beetroot, shredded
- 1 large brown onion, chopped
- 2 spring onions, chopped
- 1 tablespoon finely chopped ginger
- 2 tablespoons Chinese wine
- 1 tablespoon light soy sauce
- 1 teaspoon dark soy sauce
- freshly ground black pepper
- 2 teaspoons sesame oil
- lotus leaves (optional)
- 450 g (1lb) shortcrust pastry dough

Clean and prepare the chicken and rub the skin and the inside with salt, then set aside. Soak the mushrooms in warm water for 20 minutes, then discard the hard stems and shred the caps.

Heat the oil in a wok and stir-fry the pork for 2 minutes, then add vegetables, wine, soy sauce and pepper and cook over a moderate heat for 2-3 minutes, stirring frequently.

Stir in the sesame oil, then remove mixture with a slotted spoon and set aside to cool, then stuff into the chicken. Wrap the chicken in lotus leaves (if using) and encase in the pastry dough.

Bake in a moderately slow oven, until the chicken is tender, about 3 hours, then discard the dough and leaves and transfer to a serving plate.

Drunken Chicken

INGREDIENTS

1.5 kilos (3 ½ lb) whole chicken
25 mm (1 inch) knob fresh ginger, finely sliced
2 spring onions, sliced
900 ml (1 ½ pints) chicken stock
1 teaspoon white pepper
300 ml (10 fl oz) Chinese wine

Prepare the chicken and place in a cooking pot. Add the ginger, spring onion and stock and bring to the boil. Boil for 5 minutes, then lower heat and allow to simmer until the chicken is tender.

Remove and chop the chicken into bite-size pieces (on bone). Place in a shallow dish, season with salt and pepper and add the wine. Cover the dish with foil and place in the refrigerator for 36 hours, turning the chicken occasionally. Serve cold.

Pigeons Baked in Salt

INGREDIENTS

2 plump pigeons
4 shallots, finely chopped
4 spring onions, finely chopped
1 tablespoon finely chopped ginger
2 teaspoons finely chopped garlic
½ teaspoon ground anise
½ teaspoon five-spice powder
2 tablespoons Chinese wine
1 tablespoon light soy sauce
2 teaspoons dark soy sauce
½ teaspoon freshly ground pepper
2 kilos (4½ lbs) rock salt

Clean and prepare the pigeons. Mix together all the remaining ingredients, apart from the rock salt, and stuff inside the birds. Set aside for 1 hour, then wrap the birds individually in well-oiled baking parchment.

Heat the rock salt in a wok until it is extremely hot, then transfer half to a fresh pre-heated wok, add the pigeons and cover with remaining salt. Place a tightly-fitting lid on the wok and set aside for 10–12 minutes. Remove birds and reheat the salt, then repeat the process.

Unwrap and chop the pigeons into bite-size pieces, then place on a platter and serve with a chilli vinegar dip.

Minced Pigeon

INGREDIENTS

2 plump pigeons
100 g (4 oz) chicken livers
2 eggs
2 tablespoons light soy sauce
1 tablespoon cornflour
1 teaspoon sugar
½ teaspoon freshly ground pepper
4 dried Chinese mushrooms
4 tablespoons peanut oil
75 g (3 oz) bamboo shoots, finely chopped
3 spring onions, finely chopped
2 teaspoons finely chopped ginger
2 tablespoons Chinese wine
2 teaspoons oyster sauce
lettuce leaves
hoi sin sauce

Clean and prepare the pigeons and boil for 30–35 minutes, until tender, then allow to cool, de-bone and place through a coarse mincer. Blanch the chicken livers in boiling water, then chop finely and add to the meat.

Beat the eggs with the soy sauce, cornflour, sugar and pepper and pour over the meat. Set aside for 20 minutes, then remove with a slotted spoon and drain. Reserve the marinade.

Soak the mushrooms in warm water for 20 minutes, then discard the hard stems and finely chop the caps.

Heat the oil in a wok, add the mushroom, bamboo shoot, spring onion and ginger and stir-fry for 2 minutes, then add the wine, oyster sauce and marinade and bring to the boil.

Add the meat, adjust seasonings, and cook, stirring frequently, for 2 minutes, then transfer to a platter and serve with crispy lettuce leaves and hoi sin sauce.

Beef with Green Peppers

INGREDIENTS

400 g (14 oz) lean beef steak
1 egg white, lightly whisked with
   2 teaspoons dark soy sauce
1 tablespoon peanut oil
1 teaspoon cornflour
salt and pepper to taste
125 ml (4 fl oz) vegetable oil
2 green peppers, sliced
2 fresh red chillies, shredded
1 teaspoon minced garlic
1 tablespoon Chinese wine
1 tablespoon light soy sauce
2 teaspoons hot sesame oil

Cut the beef into thin slices and place in a shallow dish. Add the egg, stir to coat evenly and set aside for 30 minutes.

Heat the oil until it starts to smoke, then lower heat slightly and fry the beef for 45 seconds, then remove with a slotted spoon and drain on kitchen paper.

Pour away most of the oil, reheat the wok, add the pepper, chilli and garlic and stir-fry for 2 minutes, then replace the beef, add the wine and soy sauce and continue to stir for a further minute.

Transfer to a serving dish and sprinkle with hot sesame oil.

Minced Beef Balls

INGREDIENTS

400 g (14 oz) lean minced beef
125 g (4 oz) can water chestnuts,
   drained and very finely chopped
2 teaspoons finely chopped coriander
2 teaspoons Chinese wine
1/2 teaspoon salt
1/2 teaspoon freshly ground pepper
2 tablespoons cornflour
oil for deep frying

Combine the beef, water chestnut, coriander, wine, salt, pepper, half the cornflour and a little cold water and mix well to produce a thick, sticky paste.

Divide the mixture and shape with lightly floured hands into small balls, approximately 25 mm (1 inch) in diameter. Dust with the remaining cornflour and place in the refrigerator for 1 hour.

Heat the oil in a wok until it starts to smoke, then lower the heat slightly and fry the meat balls, a few at a time, for 2-3 minutes, then remove with a slotted spoon and drain on kitchen paper.

Beef in Oyster Sauce

400 g lean beef

1 egg white

2 tablespoons Chinese wine

1 tablespoon light soy sauce

2 teaspoons cornflour

½ teaspoon freshly ground pepper

4 dried Chinese mushrooms

3 tablespoons peanut oil

2 teaspoons finely chopped ginger

1 teaspoon minced garlic

1 carrot, shredded

3 tablespoons oyster sauce

1 tablespoon finely sliced spring onion

Cut the beef into thin, bite-size pieces and place in a shallow dish. Whisk the egg white together with the wine, soy sauce, cornflour and pepper and pour over the meat. Stir to coat evenly, then set aside for 30 minutes.

Soak the mushrooms in warm water for 20 minutes, then discard the hard stems and shred the caps.

Heat the oil in a wok, add the ginger and garlic and stir-fry for 2 minutes, then add the carrot and mushroom and continue to stir for a further minute.

Add the beef, remaining marinade, oyster sauce and bring to the boil. Lower heat and simmer for 1 minute, then add the spring onion and stir well.

Beef in Taro Nest

INGREDIENTS

300 g (10 oz) shredded beef
1/2 teaspoon salt
1/4 teaspoon freshly ground pepper
1/4 teaspoon five-spice powder
2 tablespoons Chinese wine
300 g (10 oz) taro root, peeled and shredded
1 egg, lightly whisked with
   1 tablespoon cornflour
vegetable oil for deep frying
1 onion, finely chopped
1 small green pepper, finely shredded
2 fresh red chillies, shredded
2 teaspoons finely chopped ginger
1 teaspoon finely chopped garlic
1 teaspoon sugar
2 tablespoons light soy sauce
2 teaspoons dark soy sauce
2 teaspoons oyster sauce
50 ml (2 fl oz) beef stock

Place the beef in a shallow dish and season with salt, pepper, five-spice powder and wine, then stir and set aside for 20 minutes. Combine the taro and egg and divide into equal portions, then arrange each portion between two wire strainers.

Heat oil in a wok until it starts to smoke, then immerse the taro and fry until crispy. Drain off excess oil, carefully remove taro from strainers and arrange on a platter.

Heat 3 tablespoons oil in a clean wok and stir-fry the beef for 1 minute, then remove and drain on kitchen paper.

Add the onion, pepper, chilli, ginger and garlic to the wok and stir-fry for 2 minutes, then add the sugar, soy sauce, oyster sauce and stock and bring to the boil. Replace the beef and stir for a further minute, then transfer to the taro nests and serve.

Spiced Beef with Bean Curd

INGREDIENTS

300 g (10 oz) minced beef
1 tablespoon Chinese wine
2 teaspoons dark soy sauce
1/4 teaspoon salt
1/4 teaspoon freshly ground pepper
150 ml (5 fl oz) peanut oil
125 g (4 oz) fresh bean curd
   cut into small cubes
2 shallots, finely chopped
4 fresh red chillies, finely chopped
1 tablespoon finely chopped ginger
1 teaspoon minced garlic
1 tablespoon fermented black beans
1 tablespoon chilli sauce
75 ml (3 oz) beef stock
2 teaspoons cornflour
1 teaspoon sesame oil
freshly chopped spring onions

Season the beef with wine, soy sauce, salt and pepper and set aside for 20 minutes.

Heat the oil in a wok until very hot and deep-fry the bean curd for 2-3 minutes, then remove with a slotted spoon and drain on kitchen paper.

Pour away most of the oil and reheat the wok. Add the shallot, chilli, ginger and garlic and stir-fry for 3 minutes, then add the beef and black beans and continue to stir over a high heat for a further 2 minutes.

Add the chilli sauce and stock and bring to the boil, then lower heat and simmer for 2 minutes. Mix the cornflour with a little cold water and stir in to thicken slightly, then replace the bean curd and sprinkle in the sesame oil.

Stir well and cook for a final minute, then transfer to a serving dish and garnish with freshly chopped spring onion.

Beef with Crispy Fried Batter

INGREDIENTS

300 g (10 oz) lean beef steak
1/4 teaspoon salt
1/4 teaspoon white pepper
1 tablespoon Chinese wine
2 tablespoons cornflour
3 tablespoons peanut oil
1 tablespoon finely chopped shallot
1 tablespoon finely chopped ginger
1 egg, lightly whisked with
   1 tablespoon light soy sauce
   1 teaspoon dark soy sauce
1/2 teaspoon sugar
75 ml (3 fl oz) beef stock
4 spring onions, finely chopped
150 g (5 oz) crispy-fried batter,
   cut into small cubes
1 teaspoon hot sesame oil

Slice the beef into thin, bite-size slices and place in a shallow dish. Season with salt and pepper and sprinkle on the wine and half the cornflour, then set aside for 30 minutes.

Heat the oil in a wok and stir-fry the beef over a moderate heat for 1 minute, then remove and drain on kitchen paper.

Reheat the wok and add the shallot and ginger. Stir-fry for 2 minutes, then add the egg, sugar and stock and bring to the boil. Add half the spring onion and replace the beef and stir for a further minute, then add the crispy batter, stir and cook for 2 minutes.

Mix the remaining cornflour with a little cold water and stir into the sauce to thicken slightly, then transfer to a serving dish. Sprinkle the hot sesame oil over the beef and garnish with the remaining spring onion.

Braised Beef with Turnips

INGREDIENTS

650 g (1¼ lbs) beef topside
½ teaspoon salt
¼ teaspoon freshly ground pepper
300 g (10 oz) turnips
3 tablespoons vegetable oil
25 mm (1 inch) knob ginger, finely sliced
2 teaspoons finely chopped garlic
1 teaspoon soybean paste
2 teaspoons finely chopped chilli
1 tablespoon Chinese wine
1 tablespoon light soy sauce
2 teaspoons dark soy sauce
1 tablespoon oyster sauce
1 teaspoon sugar
2 teaspoons cornflour

Cut the beef into large chunks and season with salt and pepper. Cut the turnips into bite-size wedges.

Heat half the oil in a wok, add the beef and stir-fry for 2 minutes to seal completely, then remove and set aside.

Heat the remaining oil in a clay cooking pot, add the ginger, garlic and bean paste and stir-fry for 3 minutes. Add the beef and cook over a high heat for a further minute, stirring continuously, then add the chilli, pour in just sufficient water to cover the beef and bring to the boil.

Lower heat, cover the pot with a tightly fitting lid and allow to cook slowly for 1½ hours, then remove lid, bring back to a fast boil and add the turnips, wine, soy sauce, oyster sauce and sugar. Again, lower heat and adjust seasonings to taste, then allow to simmer for 15-20 minutes.

Finally, mix the cornflour with a small quantity of cold water and stir into the sauce to thicken slightly, then serve immediately.

Pork Spareribs with Black Bean Sauce

INGREDIENTS

700 g (1 ½ lbs) pork spareribs
salt and black pepper
¼ teaspoon five-spice powder
3 tablespoons vegetable oil
1 tablespoon finely chopped shallot
2 teaspoons finely chopped ginger
2 teaspoon minced garlic
3 tablespoons fermented
   black beans, mashed
2 fresh red chillies, finely chopped
1 small green pepper, chopped
1 carrot, chopped
1 tablespoon Chinese wine
1 tablespoon light soy sauce
1 teaspoon dark soy sauce
1 teaspoon sugar
1 teaspoon hot sesame oil

Chop the ribs into 4 cm (1½ inch lengths) and season with salt, pepper and five-spice powder.

Heat the oil in a wok, add the shallot, ginger and garlic and stir-fry for 2 minutes, then add the ribs and stir for a further minute.

Add the black beans and continue to cook over a moderate heat for 3 minutes, stirring frequently, then add 200 ml (7 fl oz) water and bring to the boil.

Reduce heat, cover and cook for 5 minutes, then remove cover, add the chilli, green pepper and carrot. Stir for 2 minutes, then add the wine, soy sauce and sugar and bring back to a rapid boil.

Cook for a final 2 minutes, then transfer to a serving dish and sprinkle with hot sesame oil.

Pork Fillet with Lemon Sauce

INGREDIENTS

4 pork loin fillets
   approximately 150 g (5 oz) each
¼ teaspoon salt
¼ teaspoon white pepper
4 egg yolks
2 tablespoons light soy sauce
2 tablespoons Chinese wine
2 tablespoons cornflour
oil for deep frying
freshly sliced lemon

LEMON SAUCE

2 tablespoons butter
2 tablespoons plain flour
75 ml (3 fl oz) fresh lemon juice
75 ml (3 fl oz) chicken stock
2 tablespoons Chinese wine
2 teaspoons dark soy sauce
2 teaspoons sugar
salt and pepper to taste
2 teaspoons cornflour

Lay the pork fillets in a shallow dish and season with salt and pepper. Whisk the egg yolks with the soy sauce, wine and half the cornflour and pour over the meat. Stir to coat evenly and set aside for 30 minutes, then remove the fillets and dust with remaining cornflour.

Heat the oil in a wok until it starts to smoke, then lower heat slightly, add the fillets and cook until tender, golden and crispy. Remove and drain on kitchen paper, then arrange on a serving dish, cover with sauce and garnish with lemon slices.

To make the sauce, melt the butter in a small saucepan, add the flour and blend until smooth. Over a moderate heat, add the lemon juice and stock and slowly bring to the boil, stirring continuously.

Add the wine, soy sauce and sugar, season to taste with salt and pepper and stir for a further minute. Finally, mix the cornflour with a little cold water and stir into the sauce to thicken slightly.

Sweet and Sour Pork

INGREDIENTS

450 g (1 lb) pork tenderloin
½ teaspoon salt
¼ teaspoon freshly ground pepper
¼ teaspoon five-spice powder
2 eggs, lightly whisked with
 1 tablespoon Chinese wine
 1 tablespoon light soy sauce
 2 teaspoons dark soy sauce
2 tablespoons cornflour
oil for deep frying

SAUCE

2 tablespoons peanut oil
1 large onion, chopped
1 green pepper, chopped
1 tablespoon shredded ginger
1 teaspoon finely chopped garlic
1 large tomato, chopped
2 carrots, sliced
100 g (4 oz) cucumber, sliced
3 fresh red chillies, shredded
200 ml (7 fl oz) chicken stock
1 tablespoon Chinese wine
1 tablespoon light soy sauce
1 tablespoon vinegar
1 tablespoon fresh lemon juice
2 tablespoons sugar
100 g (4 oz) pineapple chunks
2 teaspoons cornflour

Cut the pork into bite-size pieces and place in a shallow dish. Season with salt, pepper and five-spice powder, then add the egg mixture and stir to coat evenly. Set aside to marinate for 30 minutes, then remove and dust with cornflour.

Heat the oil in a large wok until it starts to smoke, then lower the heat slightly, add the pork and fry for 3-4 minutes until it is well cooked and the outside is golden and crispy.

Remove the meat and drain on kitchen paper, then transfer to a serving dish and coat with sauce.

To make the sauce, pour away most of the oil from the wok and reheat, then add the onion, pepper, ginger and garlic and stir-fry for 2 minutes.

Add the tomato, carrot, cucumber and chilli and stir for a further minute, then add the stock, wine, soy sauce, vinegar, lemon juice and sugar and bring to the boil. Simmer for 2 minutes, then add the pineapple and stir for a further minute.

Finally, mix the cornflour with a small quantity of cold water and stir into the sauce to thicken slightly.

Pork Rolls with Cabbage

INGREDIENTS

350 g (12 oz) lean minced pork
1/2 teaspoon salt
1/2 teaspoon white pepper
1 teaspoon dark soy sauce
2 eggs, lightly whisked with
   2 teaspoons cornflour
3 tablespoons vegetable oil
200 g (7 oz) Chinese cabbage,
   coarsely chopped
150 ml (5 fl oz) chicken stock

Combine the pork, salt, pepper, soy sauce and egg in a bowl, then turn on a lightly-floured surface and shape into small rolls.

Heat the oil in a wok and fry the pork rolls until cooked and golden, then remove and drain on kitchen paper. Pour away half the oil, then reheat the wok, add the cabbage and stir-fry for 2 minutes. Add the stock and bring to the boil, then replace the pork, adjust seasonings to taste and cook for a further minute.

Remove the pork and the cabbage with a slotted spoon and transfer to a warm serving dish.

Bring the sauce back to the boil and reduce by half, then pour over the pork and serve immediately.

Pork with Straw Mushrooms

INGREDIENTS

500 g (1 1/2 lb) pork loin
1 tablespoon light soy sauce
2 tablespoons Chinese wine
1 teaspoon salt
1/4 teaspoon black pepper
2 tablespoons cornflour
225 g (8 oz) can straw mushrooms
2 tablespoons peanut oil
2 teaspoons finely chopped ginger
1 teaspoon finely chopped garlic
3 tablespoons chicken stock
1 tablespoon oyster sauce
2 tablespoons chopped spring onion

Cut the pork into thin, bite-size slices and place in a shallow dish. Combine the soy sauce, half the wine, the salt, pepper and half the cornflour and pour over the pork. Stir to coat evenly and set aside for 20 minutes.

Slice the mushrooms, blanch in boiling water for 30 seconds, then drain in a colander.

Heat 2 tablespoons of oil in a wok and stir fry the pork for 2-3 minutes until golden, then remove and drain on kitchen paper.

Wipe the wok, add the remaining oil and stir-fry the ginger and garlic for 3 minutes, then replace the pork, add the mushrooms and cook over a high heat for 1 minute. Add the stock, oyster sauce and remaining wine and bring to the boil.

Mix the remining cornflour with a little cold water and add to the sauce. Lower heat and allow to simmer for a further 2 minutes, then transfer to a serving dish and sprinkle the finely chopped spring onion on top.

Sweet and Sour Pork Rolls

INGREDIENTS

300 g (10 oz) pork fillet, shredded
150 g (5 oz) pork fat, finely chopped
150 g (5 oz) water chestnuts,
    finely chopped
2 tablespoons freshly chopped coriander
2 teaspoons sugar
1 teaspoon five-spice powder
1/2 teaspoon salt
1/2 teaspoon freshly ground pepper
1 tablespoon cornflour
200 ml (7 fl oz) peanut oil
1 small red pepper, chopped
1 small green pepper, chopped
100 ml (4 fl oz) rice vinegar
2 tablespoons tomato ketchup
2 teaspoon dark soy sauce
100 g (4 oz) pineapple chunks
2 teaspoons white sesame seeds

Combine the pork, pork fat, chestnut, coriander, sugar, five-spice powder, salt and pepper, then place on a piece of muslin cloth and shape into a roll, approximately 25 mm (1 inch) in diameter. Cook in steamer for 10 minutes, then allow to cool and remove the muslin. Slice into 25 mm (1 inch) pieces, shape with the hands and dust with the cornflour.

Heat the oil in a wok and fry the pork rolls for 2-3 minutes, until golden, then remove and drain on kitchen paper. Pour away most of the oil, then reheat the wok, add the red and green pepper and stir-fry for 2 minutes. Add the vinegar, ketchup and soy sauce, adjust seasonings to taste and bring to the boil.

Lower heat slightly, then add the pineapple and replace the pork. Stir for a further 2 minutes, then transfer to a serving dish and sprinkle with sesame seeds.

Dry Fried Green Beans

INGREDIENTS

450 g (1 lb) string beans

125 g (4 oz) fresh shrimps

oil for deep frying

75 g (3 oz) minced pork

2 teaspoons finely chopped ginger

1 teaspoon minced garlic

75 g (3 oz) pickled vegetables, finely chopped

2 teaspoons sugar

1/2 teaspoon freshly ground pepper

1 tablespoon light soy sauce

75 ml (3 oz) chicken stock

2 teaspoons vinegar

2 fresh red chillies, finely sliced

Top and tail the beans and cut into 5 cm (2 inch) lengths. Shell and de-vein the shrimps and chop finely.

Heat the oil in a wok until it starts to smoke and fry the beans for 2-3 minutes, then remove with a slotted spoon and drain on kitchen paper. Pour away the oil and wipe the wok with a dry cloth. Replace the beans and stir over a high heat until they start to blacken, then remove and set aside.

Add 2 tablespoons of fresh oil to the wok and reheat, then add the shrimp, pork, ginger, garlic and pickle and stir-fry for 2-3 minutes. Add the sugar, pepper, soy sauce and stock and bring to the boil, then replace the beans. Retain over a high heat, stirring frequently, until the liquid has evaporated. Stir in the vinegar and cook for a further 30 seconds, then transfer the beans to a serving plate and garnish with the sliced chilli.

Sweet and Sour Cabbage

INGREDIENTS

600 g (1 1/4 lb) Chinese cabbage

4 fresh red chillies, chopped finely

4 tablespoons vegetable oil

2 tablespoons finely chopped smoked ham

1 teaspoon black peppercorns, coarsely crushed

1/2 teaspoon salt

2 teaspoons sugar

1 tablespoon dark soy sauce

4 tablespoons vinegar

1 tablespoon sesame oil

Tear the cabbage leaves into pieces and finely chop the spines.

Heat the oil in a saucepan and stir-fry the chillies until they start to blacken, then add the cabbage, ham and crushed pepper and cook for 3-4 minutes, until the cabbage is soft.

Add the salt, sugar and soy sauce and cook for a further minute, then remove pan from the heat, add the vinegar and sesame oil and stir to blend thoroughly.

Stir-Fried Mixed Vegetables

INGREDIENTS

1 small onion, chopped

2 shallots, chopped

1 teaspoon minced garlic

60 ml (2 fl oz) peanut oil

3 fresh red chillies, finely chopped

200 g (7 oz) cauliflower florets

125 g (4 oz) green beans, sliced

6 carrots, sliced

1 green pepper, chopped

1 tablespoon Chinese wine

1 tablespoon light soy sauce

3 tablespoons chicken stock

freshly ground black pepper

Combine the onion, shallot, garlic and 1 teaspoon oil and pound to produce a smooth paste.

Heat the remaining oil in a wok, add the paste and stir-fry for 3–4 minutes, then add all the vegetables and continue to stir for a further for 4–5 minutes.

Add the wine, soy sauce, stock and pepper and bring to the boil. Cook for a further minute, then transfer to a serving dish.

Stuffed Mushrooms

INGREDIENTS

12 dried Chinese mushrooms

1 teaspoon sugar

¼ teaspoon black pepper

½ teaspoon salt

1 tablespoon Chinese wine

2 teaspoons sesame oil

200 g (7 oz) fresh shrimps

2 teaspoons cornflour

2 tablespoons finely chopped Yunnan ham

fresh coriander leaves

Soak the mushrooms in warm water for 20 minutes, then pat dry and remove the hard stems. Place the caps in a shallow dish, sprinkle with the sugar, pepper and half the salt, wine and sesame oil. Steam for 10 minutes, then set aside to cool.

Shell and de-vein the shrimps and chop finely, then pound with the cornflour and remaining salt, wine and oil to produce a smooth paste. Spread the paste on the inside of the mushrooms, then sprinkle with chopped ham.

Steam the mushrooms for a further 10 minutes, then transfer to a serving dish and garnish with fresh coriander leaves.

Mushrooms with Bean Curd

INGREDIENTS

6 dried Chinese mushrooms

300 g (10 oz) fresh bean curd

250 ml (8 fl oz) vegetable oil

2 shallots, finely chopped

2 teaspoons finely chopped ginger

1 teaspoon minced garlic

1 teaspoon sugar

½ teaspoon freshly ground pepper

1 tablespoon Chinese wine

1 tablespoon light soy sauce

125 ml (4 fl oz) chicken stock

2 teaspoons cornflour

Soak the mushrooms in warm water for 20 minutes, then discard the hard stems and cut the caps in half. Soak the bean curd in cold water for 3 minutes, then drain and cut into bite-size pieces.

Heat the oil in a wok until it starts to smoke, then add the bean curd and fry until golden. Remove with a slotted spoon and drain on kitchen paper. Pour away all but 2 tablespoons oil and reheat the wok, then add the shallot, ginger and garlic and stir-fry for 2 minutes.

Add the mushrooms and continue to stir for a further 2 minutes, then add the sugar, pepper, wine, soy sauce and stock and bring to the boil. Lower heat and replace the bean curd, then allow to simmer for 3 minutes.

Finally, mix the cornflour with a small quantity of cold water and stir into the sauce to thicken slightly, then transfer to a warm dish and serve immediately.

Chilli Bean Curd

INGREDIENTS

300 g (10 oz) fresh bean curd
2 tablespoons peanut oil
100 g (4 oz) minced pork
2 shallots, finely chopped
6 fresh red chillies, finely sliced
1 tablespoon finely chopped ginger
2 teaspoons finely chopped garlic
2 teaspoons hot bean paste
1 tablespoon light soy sauce
2 teaspoons dark soy sauce
1 tablespoon Chinese wine
175 ml (6 fl oz) chicken stock
freshly ground black pepper
2 spring onions, finely chopped

Soak the bean curd in cold water for 3 minutes, then drain and cut into chunks.

Heat the oil in a wok and stir-fry the pork for 3-4 minutes, then remove with a slotted spoon and drain on kitchen paper.

Reheat the oil, add the shallot, chilli, ginger and garlic and stir-fry for 3 minutes.

Replace the pork, add the bean paste, soy sauce, wine and stock and bring to the boil, then lower heat, add the bean curd and season to taste with black pepper.

Continue to cook, stirring frequently, for a further 3-4 minutes, then transfer to a serving dish and garnish with finely chopped spring onion.

Aubergine in Hot Garlic Sauce

INGREDIENTS

350 g (12 oz) aubergine
150 ml (5 fl oz) peanut oil
4 fresh red chillies, finely chopped
1 tablespoon finely chopped ginger
1 tablespoon minced garlic
75 g (3 oz) minced beef
2 spring onions, finely sliced
1 teaspoon sugar
1 tablespoon Chinese wine
1 tablespoon light soy sauce
100 ml (4 fl oz) chicken stock
2 teaspoons vinegar
1 teaspoon sesame oil

Trim and wash the aubergine and cut into finger-size pieces. Heat the oil in a wok and fry the aubergine for 2 minutes, then remove and squeeze out excess oil.

Pour away most of the oil and re-heat the wok, then add the chilli, ginger and garlic and stir-fry for 2 minutes. Add the beef and spring onion and cook for a further minute, then add the sugar, wine, soy sauce and stock and bring to the boil.

Lower heat to moderate, then replace the aubergine, adjust seasonings to taste and continue to cook, stirring occasionally, until the liquid has reduced by two-thirds. Finally, add the vinegar and sesame oil and stir well, then transfer to a serving dish.

Cabbage and Water Chestnuts

INGREDIENTS

450 g (1 lb) Chinese cabbage

75 g (3 oz) straw mushrooms

125 g (4 oz) water chestnuts, thinly sliced

75 ml (3 fl oz) vegetable oil

400 ml (14 oz) chicken stock

1 teaspoon sugar

salt and freshly ground pepper

2 teaspoons finely chopped ginger

1 teaspoon minced garlic

2 tablespoons Chinese wine

2 tablespoons oyster sauce

2 teaspoons cornflour

2 spring onions, finely chopped

Discard the stem and outside leaves and cut the cabbage into serving-size pieces, then blanch in boiling water for 1 minute. Blanch the mushrooms for 1 minute.

Heat 3 tablespoons of oil in a wok and stir-fry the cabbage and mushrooms for 1 minute, then remove and drain on kitchen paper. Add the chestnuts and stir-fry until golden, then remove and drain. Discard the oil and wipe the wok clean. Add 300 ml (10 fl oz) of stock to the wok and bring to the boil, then replace vegetables, add the sugar and season to taste with salt and pepper. Reduce the heat, cover the wok and allow to simmer for 5-7 minutes, then remove and drain. Discard liquid.

Add remaining oil to the wok and stir-fry the ginger and garlic for 3 minutes, then add the wine, oyster sauce and remaining stock. Bring to the boil, replace the vegetables and stir for 2 minutes. Finally, mix the cornflour with a little water and stir into the sauce to thicken, then transfer to serving dish and garnish with finely chopped spring onion.

Broccoli in Wine Sauce

INGREDIENTS

250 g (9 oz) broccoli florets

300 ml (10 fl oz) vegetable oil

500 ml (1 1/4 pints) chicken stock

1 small lettuce, shredded

2 tablespoons peanut oil

2 teaspoons shredded ginger

1 teaspoon minced garlic

2 tablespoons Chinese wine

1 tablespoon oyster sauce

1 tablespoon light soy sauce

1 teaspoon dark soy sauce

1 tablespoon finely chopped ham

Wash the broccoli and pat dry. Heat the vegetable oil in a wok and deep-fry the broccoli for 2 minutes, then remove and drain on kitchen paper.

Place 300 ml (10 fl oz) stock in a saucepan and bring to the boil. Add the lettuce and cook for 1 minute, then remove with a slotted spoon and place in the bottom of a serving dish. Add the broccoli to the stock and simmer for 2 minutes, then remove, drain and place on top of the lettuce.

Meanwhile, heat the peanut oil in a small pan and stir-fry the ginger and garlic for 2 minutes. Add the wine, oyster sauce, soy sauce and remaining stock and bring to the boil. Mix the cornflour with a small quantity of cold water and add to the stock. Stir until the sauce thickens, then pour over the broccoli and sprinkle with the chopped ham.

Braised Vegetable Casserole

INGREDIENTS

6 dried Chinese mushrooms
75 g (3 oz) dried wood ear mushrooms
150 g (5 oz) aubergine
150 g (5 oz) white cabbage
150 g (5 oz) broccoli
150 g (5 oz) bok choi
2 carrots
1 green pepper
125 g can bamboo shoots, drained
75 ml (3 fl oz) vegetable oil
100 g (4 oz) bean curd, thinly sliced
1 teaspoon finely chopped garlic
1 teaspoon finely chopped ginger
1 teaspoon finely chopped red chilli
1 teaspoon sugar
1 tablespoon light soy sauce
1 tablespoon oyster sauce

Soak the mushrooms in 400 ml warm water for 20 minutes, then discard the hard stems and halve the caps. Soak the wood ear mushrooms for 30 minutes, then slice thinly. Retain the water. Prepare the vegetables and cut into bite-size pieces. Heat half the oil in a wok and fry the bean curd until golden, then remove and drain. Add the vegetables to the wok and stir-fry for 1 minute, then remove and drain.

Heat a large clay pot over a fairly high heat, then add remaining oil. Allow to become very hot, then add the garlic and ginger and stir for 1 minute. Add the chilli, sugar, soy sauce, oyster sauce and reserved water and bring to the boil. Add the vegetables, cover the pot and cook for 4–5 minutes, then add the bean curd, adjust seasonings to taste and cook for a further 2-3 minutes.

Bean Paste Meringues

INGREDIENTS

5 egg whites

4 heaped tablespoons custard powder

3 tablespoons castor sugar

1/2 teaspoon red food colouring

125 g (4 oz) sweet bean paste

1 1/2 tablespoons cornflour

oil for deep frying

Beat the egg whites in a bowl until fairly stiff, then blend in the custard powder and continue to beat until the mixture is very firm. Combine the sugar and food colouring and set to one side.

Mix the bean paste with a small quantity of cold water and shape into marble-size balls. Dust these with cornflour and dip into the egg mixture, allowing a considerable amount to stick; the finished meringue should be approximately 5 cm (2 inches) in diameter.

Heat the oil in a large wok until it starts to`smoke, then lower heat slightly and deep-fry the meringues for approximately 2 minutes. Remove with a slotted spoon and drain off excess oil, then roll in the coloured sugar and serve immediately.

Date Pancakes

INGREDIENTS

150 g (5 oz) pitted dates, finely chopped

150 g (5 oz) granulated sugar

100 g (4 oz) sweet bean paste

oil for deep frying

6 pancakes

egg wash

3 tablespoons icing sugar

Place the dates and sugar in a saucepan, add just sufficient water to cover and bring to the boil, then lower the heat and simmer for 5 minutes, stirring frequently. Remove and allow to cool, then press the mixture through a fine sieve and combine with the bean paste.

Heat 2 tablespoons of oil in a wok and stir-fry the mixture over a moderate heat for 5 minutes, then remove and drain. Spoon portions of the mixture on to the pancakes and fold the sides to secure, brush with egg wash.

Heat the remaining oil in a large wok until it starts to smoke, then lower heat slightly and deep-fry the pancakes, two at a time, until golden. Remove and drain off excess oil, then dust with icing sugar and serve immediately.

Toffee Apples and Bananas

2 apples
4 medium size bananas
150 g (5 oz) plain flour
large pinch of salt
1 egg, whisked
peanut oil for deep frying
1 tablespoon sesame seeds
150 g (5 oz) sugar
sesame oil

Peel and quarter the bananas, lengthways.
Peel and core the apples and cut each into six slices.

Sift the flour and salt into a bowl. Break the egg into a bowl, add 125 ml (4 fl oz) of cold water, and whisk well to produce a smooth batter. Dip the fruit in the batter to coat evenly.

Heat the oil in a wok until it is very hot and deep-fry the pieces of fruit until golden, then remove with a slotted spoon, drain on kitchen paper and sprinkle with sesame seeds.

Meanwhile, place the sugar and 250 ml (9 fl oz) water in a saucepan and stir gently over a moderate heat until almost caramelised.

Coat the pieces of fruit with the hot caramel syrup and plunge into a bowl of iced water. Transfer to a plate lightly coated with sesame oil and serve while the sugary coating is hard.

Almond Jelly with Fruit Salad

INGREDIENTS

2 tablespoons agar-agar powder
75 g (3 oz) sugar
1 teaspoon almond essence
150 ml (5 fl oz) condensed milk
300 g (10 oz) mixed fruit salad

Place 600 ml (1 pint) of water in a saucepan, add the agar-agar and half the sugar and bring to the boil.

Lower heat and simmer for 2 minutes, then add the almond essence, condensed milk and remaining sugar and continue to cook over a moderate heat for a further 5 minutes, stirring frequently.

Pour the mixture into a shallow, lightly-greased cake tin and allow to cool, then chill until set firmly.

Chill a serving bowl in the refrigerator, then remove, add shaved ice, jelly and fruit salad and stir gently. Serve immediately.

ABALONE

A large sea mollusk with a particularly hard shell, often seen in fish tanks outside Chinese seafood restaurants. Fresh abalone can be very expensive but the canned variety is just as good and readily available.

AGAR AGAR POWDER

A vegetarian alternative to gelatine. Made from seaweed, rich in iodine and trace minerals and with strong setting properties.

BAK CHOI

A white cabbage with a mild yet distinctive flavour. In addition to being served as a vegetable dish it is often included in soup and meat recipes.

BAMBOO SHOOTS

A cream coloured, conical shaped vegetable. When fresh, it needs to be peeled and boiled for some considerable time – simpler is the canned variety which is widely available in supermarkets.

BEAN CURD (TOFU)

Soy beans treated with an extract of rennet. Is highly nutritious as it is concentrated protein and is sold, fresh, in cubes or 'silk' form, or can be dried, freeze-dried, fermented, deep-fried and smoked. Leftover fresh bean curd can be kept in the fridge submerged in water, which must be changed every day.

BEAN PASTE

Made from a base of soy beans and available in various flavours – hot bean paste is flavoured with chillies while the sweet variety uses sugar and seasonings.

BEAN SPROUTS

The sprouts of the green mung beans. Available in Asian stores and most supermarkets. Served as a vegetable and used in many stir-fries.

BLACK BEAN SUACE

A sauce made from fermented soy beans, water and wheat flour and widely available commercially.

BLACK MUSHROOMS

Often referred to as 'Chinese' mushrooms, these are sold dried and need soaking in warm water before using. The flavour is unique and there is no acceptable substitute.

CHILLIES

Fresh chillies are used liberally in some styles of Chinese cooking, especially in dishes from the North and the Western province of Sichuan but seldom in the classical and universally popular Cantonese cuisine. Regardless of the quantities suggested in the recipes, the preference of individual palates must always be the main consideration. Fresh chillies are usually chopped or sliced, and the seeds discarded. Dried chillies require soaking in warm water before cooking unless being used whole for cooking meats and poultry, in which case they are discarded before serving.

CHOI SUM

A very popular Chinese vegetable with a slightly bitter taste, often cooked or served with oyster sauce. It has thin green stems, 'pencil-like' leaves and small yellow flowers.

CORIANDER

Also known as Chinese parlsey, the bright green leaves are used frequently in cooking and add a distinctive aromatic flavour to any dish. The seeds are readily available and usually ground with other spices before use.

DIM SUM

A collective name for small Chinese snacks, fried and steamed, traditionally served from breakfast to lunch. Sweet varieties are also popular in the afternoon and as a conclusion to an evening meal. There are hundreds of varieties, many of which are time consuming to prepare so they are more likely to be served in a restaurant than in a home.

FIVE-SPICE POWDER
A strong seasoning used a great deal in Chinese cooking and made from equal quantities of Sichuan peppercorns, fennel seeds, cinnamon bark, star anise and cloves.

GINGER
Generally bought as a root stem and peeled, then sliced, grated or ground. Fried with garlic and onion, the mixture is the base for stir-fries. Occasionally pressed to produce a ginger juice, (also used for medicinal purposes), ginger is sometimes added at the end of cooking as a condiment.

GLUTINOUS RICE
A variety of long-grain rice which becomes sticky and transparent when cooked.

HOISIN SAUCE
A sweet and spicy sauce, made from salted black beans, onions and garlic, which is often served as a side dish with meat and poultry. Available commercially.

LOTUS LEAVES
Lotus leaves are just one of the culinary benefits of the lotus plant. They are usually bought in bundles of dried leaves and need to be soaked for a couple of hours to soften them. They can then be used to wrap food such as fish, pork or poultry and then placed on a barbecue, in an oven and baked, steamed or in a soup.

OYSTER SAUCE
Made from oysters boiled in salted water and soy sauce and then thickened with starches. Available commercially. It adds a distinctive flavour to many meat and vegetable dishes.

SESAME OIL
A strong oil with a slightly nutty flavour, made from roasted sesame seeds. Very small quantities will enhance the flavour when used in cooking or in side dips. It is not used as a cooking oil.

SICHUAN PEPPERCORNS
Brown in colour, these peppercorns add a pleasant aroma and mildly hot flavour to a dish. An important ingredient of Five-Spice Powder.

SOY SAUCE
An absolute essential in every Chinese kitchen. There are many types of soy sauce, made from fermented soy beans, the most commonly used ones being a 'light' one and a 'dark' one, the latter used less frequently and more sparingly.

STAR ANISE
Commercially available as a dried, star-shaped fruit with a strong aniseed flavour and often associated with pork and poultry dishes. Also available in ground form.

WATER CHESTNUTS
Small bulbs with a tough brown skin and white flesh which add a crunchy texture to stir-fries. Widely available in cans, and will keep for some time when the water is changed regularly.

WINTER MELON
Also known as a 'wax' or 'white' gourd, the winter melon is a fast-growing, long-season, warm-climate vegetable. It is considered a Chinese comfort food.

WON TON WRAPPERS
Squares of very thin dough, made with high gluten flour and readily available in specialist Chinese stores, and some supermarkets. Used to encase various fillings for dim-sum, and also in soups.

YUNNAN HAM
This ham, processed with a lot of salt, is available either 'fresh' or in tins.

INDEX

Pork Spareribs with Black Bean Sauce 58
Pork Rolls with Cabbage 61
Pork with Straw Mushrooms 61
Spring Rolls 11
Steamed Buns with Barbecued Pork 15
Stir-Fried Pork Rolls 16
Sweet and Sour Pork 60
Sweet and Sour Pork Rolls 62
Taro Dumplings 12

PRAWNS

Crab Claws with Prawn Paste 28
Hot and Sour Soup 26
Minced Prawn Balls 8
Prawn Cutlets 31
Prawns Dumplings 8
Seafood and Bean Curd Soup 20
Sesame Prawns 31
Sesame Prawn Toast 9
Stir-Fried Prawns with Choi Sum 30
Stuffed Mushrooms 66
Won Ton Soup 19

Raw Fish Soup 22
Seafood with Bean Curd Soup 20
Sesame Prawns 6
Sesame Prawn Toast 9
Shark's Fin and Crabmeat Soup 23

SHRIMPS

Spring Rolls 11
Taro dumplings 12
Smoked Pomfret 39

SOUPS

Chicken and Sweetcorn Soup 24
Chicken Liver and Sweetcorn Soup 20
Crabmeat and Sweetcorn Soup 20
Hot and Sour Soup 26
Pork Liver and Tomato Soup 25
Seafood and Bean Curd Soup 20
Shark's Fin and Crabmeat Soup 23
Winter Melon Soup 18
Won Ton Soup 19

Spiced Beef with Bean Curd 56
Spicy Steamed Pomfret 38
Spring Rolls 11
Steamed Buns with Barbecued Pork 15
Steamed Garoupa with Ham and Mushrooms 34

Steamed Pomfret, Chiu Chow Style 36
Stir-Fried Lobster 32
Stir-Fried Mixed Vegetables 65
Stir-Fried Pork Rolls 16
Stir-Fried Prawns with Choi Sum 30
Stuffed Mushrooms 66
Stuffed Duckling 43
Sweet and Sour Cabbage 64
Sweet and Sour Fish 34
Sweet and Sour Pork 60
Sweet and Sour Pork Rolls 62
Taro Dumplings 12
Toffee Apples and Bananas 73

TOFU (See BEAN CURD)

VEGETABLES

Aubergine in Hot Garlic Sauce 68
Braised Vegetable Casserole 70
Broccoli in Wine Sauce 69
Cabbage and Water Chestnuts 69
Dry Fried Green Beans 64
Mushrooms with Bean Curd 66
Stir-Fried Mixed Vegetables 65
Stuffed Mushrooms 66
Sweet and Sour Cabbage 64

Winter Melon Soup 18